Praise for *Elephant*

What a beautiful book! These are remarkably wise poems, a festival of wisdom, and then it turns whacky and I would even say piquant. Touching is exactly the word I mean even when touch is the nullity Soren sounds. There is an abundance of the interior, Rilke being the easiest compare but Soren's dedication to how the exterior wounds the soul and the soul carries on is the gift of this work that always unwinds and continues, beautiful and beyond us. Spoiler alert! there are lots of poems in here I would call masterpiece.
—Eileen Myles

Soren Stockman's *Elephant* opens with eighteen short love poems, filled with raw passion and spirit. And then suddenly, we come to the second section, and the tone and landscape shift, slightly, into a world of the "Elephant Man," its imagistic power and mystery revealed—the other, the outcast, a human specimen to be doctored on. Indeed, love is woven into this urban space that defies time; but true "brotherly love" becomes the speaker's real quest as *Elephant* unfolds each gift.
—Yusef Komunyakaa

From the fields of Wyoming to the New York stage, Soren Stockman's poems of love and family are direct and forceful as they explore the powerful, unpayable debts that shape a self. Addiction, lust, anarchy—all are made tender in Stockman's skill and imagination. Often inspired by theater and made alive by theater's glittering and intoxicating illusions, *Elephant* shows us the beauty and pain of inhabiting a life and inhabiting a body.
—Richie Hofmann

Love is Stockman's theme, and love done well requires listening: "Some people will care for you, / you need to let them." A dramatic monologue in the voice of John Merrick, "The Elephant Man," haunts the collection. Listening maps out the poems. Cryptic

and original, Stockman turns his poems inside out by listening. Stockman writes: "I promise your gentleness has already lasted so many lives." *Elephant* read *me*. What brilliant poems.
— Spencer Reece

Tennyson insisted, *'Tis better to have loved and lost than never to have loved at all*. Soren Stockman's lovely, lovesick debut *Elephant* echoes Tennyson's sentiment for the ages, as it breaks your heart. And, like love, *Elephant* is worth it.
—Nicole Sealey

"I looked at my loneliness / and could say nothing," writes Stockman in his debut. But these pages run away from that nothingness, masterfully showcasing love, shame, and sensuality wrestling together. What a blessing *Elephant* is in the world, born ready to sing a tune that brings us out of solitude.
—Javier Zamora

Soren Stockman is a true poet who is interested in looking at the world without judging it. His debut book of poems, *Elephant*, is full of heart and reminds me that being alive is a singular experience. If you want to be reminded of that, read this book.
—Alex Dimitrov

Soren Stockman's quirky poetics lay bare a private life in *Elephant* where readers will find a closeness akin to autobiography although the details never depend on autobiography. Further, like "a crow constructs / a tool from another tool and finds its food," Stockman presents a complex revealing of the legendary Elephant Man—and how he relates to and interrelates with this figure. Welcome this debut collection and Stockman's marvelous elliptical sleight of hand.
—Kimiko Hahn

Elephant

Elephant

Soren Stockman

Four Way Books
Tribeca

*For my family, who teach me the splendor
and grace of loving and being loved, and who gave me
a place in the world.*

Library of Congress Cataloging-in-Publication Data

Names: Stockman, Soren, author.
Title: Elephant / Soren Stockman.
Description: New York : Four Way Books, [2022]
Identifiers: LCCN 2022003871 | ISBN 9781954245310 (paperback) | ISBN 9781954245402 (epub)
Subjects: LCGFT: Poetry.
Classification: LCC PS3619.T6363 E44 2022 | DDC 811/.6--dc23/eng/20220201
LC record available at https://lccn.loc.gov/2022003871

This book is manufactured in the United States of America and printed on acid-free paper.

Four Way Books is a not-for-profit literary press. We are grateful for the assistance we receive from individual donors, public arts agencies, and private foundations including the NEA, NEA Cares, Literary Arts Emergency Fund, and the New York State Council on the Arts, a state agency.

We are a proud member of the Community of Literary Magazines and Presses.

Contents

WYOMING

ELEPHANT MAN

JOSEPH MERRICK

Love bade me welcome. Yet my soul drew back
  Guilty of dust and sin.
But quick-eyed Love, observing me grow slack
  From my first entrance in,
Drew nearer to me, sweetly questioning,
  If I lacked any thing.
     —George Herbert

Only love can break your heart.
     —Neil Young

WYOMING

TO BE BORN

When I was young I was really
an old man. I remember it, delicate
and spacious: aware I would
become more honest, feel natural,
knowing half of love
is need. A serious young man,
I had trouble saying *yes*
to the bright, clear days. With what
pitiful ease we could change—
our lives out, something else in
—but the tissue holds memory
we don't quite know. One
night, like a boxer dropping
his gloves, I answered
every question immediately.
Slowly we laughed more,
we were hysterical at night
and morning blew the doors open.
I ate a radish, never contracted
chicken pox, my singing improved
and women never stopped looking.
Then my friends began to die.
They passed through the beautiful old
maples I watch from my window.
What a blessing to love the world
and then finally be born.

LOVE

A glass bottle on the side of a private road
filled with beetles and roaches. Maybe they
crawled in to nourish themselves, and late-
comers to feed on those that came before them.
Maybe they knew the bottle magnified the sun
as it killed them with heat, or maybe
they never did, climbing over each other.
In Maine, they trap lobsters by leaving food
at the far end of a cage pierced with one small hole.
The lobsters find a way in (maybe they eat,
maybe they don't), and never find the way out.

HERE

A spot of blood in my tea.

You on my weighted lip.

Fissure I can find, I can be.

Apart from any dragonfly,

apart from a sudden rain

is this, and more fragrant,

more. Incantation of my own.

I stir it in. *You,* and the bright,

bright moon. The dock floats.

A light burst lithe, like

stars imploding far

in quiet hours. More quiet

than deer sleeping, than grass

underneath them, is this.

Glass waves go

in motion and between.

Easy, now. Even here

is a long time away.

HOW TWO DRAGONFLIES, HAVING CIRCLED

each other and found each other ideal
in unromantic terms, become attached
mid-air, and stop to alight on one lily
or its stem, and stay there together perfectly
still. And, once they have finished
their unromantic, ideal business, how
one departs and the other remains, circling
that lily a long time, as though looking
for another in place of itself.

BURYING ANGELS

A wing comes off, so I keep it on my table.
I lay down on the carpet, looking.
Another dead. Another.
Trying to bury them. Extremely unsure
of myself. The head comes off, the wing.
Before I can decide not to, I blow
them clumsily toward the grate.
Kneeling, my face an inch from the ground,
moving about the room like this,
I search for hours.

A HUGE MEADOW

All the past is not a diminishing road but, instead, a
huge meadow which no winter ever quite touches...

—William Faulkner

As the beloved is ensnared by the lover,
he dimly recognizes he is caught
though he cannot see the trap. Either
too dark or too bright. Who knew orange
was next to gray, black and brown, but
the tawny mountains. Not the cattle
making their way slowly up the hillsides.
The great gift of first failing in love.
The vow never to do it again, against
every principle he thought he had
wrapped tight around him. Past
the mountains, emerging suddenly
into a huge meadow. The vessel quakes,
too small for the cargo, and lies down
as fast as it can. Familiar deer
quietly summon him to a new place,
and do not watch him anymore, permitting
his transformation into landscape.

THE ANIMAL

And if wind runs through
      leaves on each tree like a brush

and night exhales the sound
      of water   I hear myself breathe

And if I wake in the middle of the night
      my head throbbing   and if

I touch myself   not knowing what
      to do   and the pain leaves   if only

until the morning   what have I
done   thinking of no one

If the voices I hear outside
my window cease   I am kept

awake by a deeper silence
I cannot touch   Cobwebs mingle

with what spiders have made

and the trees keep   dropping
the seeds from which they came

if only in my imagination   if only
at first   before I see the animal

the animal is real

APPLES

Failure is the temptation of the strong, the bones
of the weak, and everything to everyone
in between. The clamor as I enter into silence.
Failure must be perfect, perfection the salvation
offered under my beaten table. When I fail,
I fail as my perfect incarnation.

It is the trust I have constructed, like a summer
home for the poor. The apples for free
in the orchard, the wealthy ordering them
across the country. Two ways to approach
failure, from either side. The solemn
retreat into it, and the aggressive advance.

THE BIGGER FIRE

I don't know the chemistry of two fires
converging, but I know the bigger fire of not wanting
consumes the fire of wanting. I have searched
the beast's hot belly—it is incredible:
no difference between the thing and what has been
swallowed, like a bone dropped in the body.
They burn together, and as one grows, the other grows,
but you can tell which is which:
      the bigger fire reaches furthest, controls the
  surface,
holds inside it something almost peaceful.

DUSK IN WYOMING

As a woman gives birth to a child
that once was a part of her before
becoming entirely itself, violence
begets a small child named violence.

DOCTOR

Why do the deer have black eyes that glow
red in the dark, and why are the wild turkeys
so petty and stupid, pecking at each other
all the time? There's a doe that follows
her fawns across the road, and a turkey
king that puffs himself up to scare away
the other turkey kings while his harem nearby
roosts. These creatures find in the same grass
something they like, something they depend on.

I wake to pain in my ears crackling,
blood on my pillowcase, and fill
my hatred bowl with desperation,
as I do, trying to get it out of me
in the most acceptable way. I hear
the doctor ask my parents if they think
I'm an alcoholic, a memory I rely on
to hurt me further whenever I latch
onto a different pain, a separate pain.

NOTHING RECOGNIZABLE

I will show it to you once it is safely mine

said the thing I love in everyone

AFTERNOON IN WYOMING

Deer have begun to cross the fields,
which means it is the first of three
times they will graze today. If I

open the door, they will turn toward me,
perfect in stillness. If I move after that,
they will dance away, their white tails . . .

I watch them through my window and try
to slow down time. Deer know where to sleep,
where it's best to drink from the stream. *Have you*

ever met a beautiful man who didn't want
to be beautiful? I ask them. *Wouldn't that be virtuous?*
A doe, her fawn trailing her, answers,

That would be stupid. Who would he be to deny
the formative godhead? What is his self-loathing
worth to him? She sighs, and the day passes.

Lint pirouettes across my eyeballs.
Yes, but it's dangerous, I reply. The doe
looks away, catching a scent, then back at me.

It's only dangerous if you're a fool. I can't believe
you're writing about this. You are not beautiful,
so you don't have to worry, okay?

I have yet to meet him anyways, I say.
The deer shake their heads and disappear.

ANGEL MADE GRAY

quickly her body
      is only a body

one vicious twist out
      and the light leaves

her skin is torn
      it will not heal

your hands shine
      you have survived her

LUSTRAL

My lust comes home. I wait for her
in a time for private imaginations.
Five years she's been gone. I missed
the ordinary time we'd spend together.
Girls I cared nothing about lay down,
and down, and loved, as a crow constructs
a tool from another tool and finds its food.
My lust comes home. Two skeletons
that cannot possibly speak, and don't,
do not, as I comfort her. Sit her
in my living room, her quiet with her.
Grip her body, uncover her sheen outside
of time. The silver buttons on her dress
mellifluous. My fingers in her mouth.

PERMISSION

Not what I always wanted, but the permission
to want it. And to make it, to make it mine,
to have been making it forever, to make it
always. Greedy that way, and lovely.

BLOOD FLOWERS

Love is a fetus that grows in my stomach.

Each morning I buy newspapers

en route to the blood bank.

I throw donations over my shoulder like salt;

I want my love to be everywhere, am sure

little losses will strengthen what is left.

Then love begins to bite through me,

calling my name in the dark, eating my body.

Placenta percreta: like the jerk and groan of muscle,

a child tunnels up through my gullet.

The umbilical cord follows, still attached,

collapsing my throat, sitting at the back of my mouth.

Soon I vomit blood flowers, and butterflies

feed on their nectar in midsummer heat.

The stem is rooted in me, a taut and milky cord.

Red petals fall backward as yellow ones emerge,

new mouths open, gaping at the world.

MORNING IN WYOMING

My whole life there have been people
who have looked at me knowingly.

Like the child who knows the hand pointing
to the moon, and not the moon itself.

The corruption of faith, the downfall
we surrender asunder.

Each night before sleep, I forgive myself.
At the end of each year, I forgive myself that.

Death will be gorgeous. There is no love
when there is nothing but love.

ELEPHANT MAN

ELEPHANT MAN

I was born to Joseph and Mary Jane and was called John.
I had the feeling I had done something wrong
but couldn't quite understand the entire context, or what
I had done, specifically, that should cause me to feel
shame that did not hold up to the hot light of my own
investigation but was exponentially aggravated
when my audience was cruel or drunk, and so my own mind's eye
transformed my shame into a mythical beast with giant
bat-like wings. I was often in hospitals, and ended by
living in one, like a hotel. I was not pretty
and because of this I thrived in my hospital home
where I lived decently in the ugliness they saw.
There was a doctor who eventually learned to be human.
There was a businessman who ran the hospital.
There was me, unable to sleep in a reclined position
because the weight of my head drew my blood
and I would die during the night. There I was
knowing to prop myself with pillows. There was
the hallway and my room at the end, where sometimes
I entertained visitors whom I loved as though
they were my very parents who had loved and cared for me
all my life, as though I were a pretty child. I was not
comfortable at aristocratic functions but accepted them
with a kindly smile. My face was not what I had done wrong,
but it felt like a simple solution to my guilt. I became famous.
It would have been nice not to be famous for being physically
hideous, having either a good or a bad light poured over me.
I had so many handlers, I cannot remember their names.
Some of them even stuck around, keeping an eye
on me and my blood flow, my lipids and my whatever else.

One who was very good, and also kind, would try
to get me into shape, but I was too expensive
to maintain. I thanked him and I felt a kind of love toward him.
I looked up to everyone because my forehead
was my most engorged body part and so it hung in front of me (I
could see its top edge if I looked straight up), though I was larger
and often taller than other freaks in the sideshow.
The little people who were my compatriots would speak to me.
We were all hysterical and high-pitched, washed clean
by the whirring fans and swollen heat and the dark red carpets
we cleaned. I kept John in my pocket like a coin my mother gave me.
My beautiful mother, whom I remember carefully. She died
and I thought I might have killed her somehow, perhaps with
    disappointment.
My handler gave me medicine. My doctor gave me society.
I dressed in a fancy coat and knew to bow in the right direction,
even when I could not see the lord presenting me
with a gift of some kind. I drew a constellation on the wall in my
    bedroom,
a church I could connect in the stars. Slowly I made the shape,
    pulling
and smudging and rubbing it across the sky wall like something
    made
from my own body that I could not control, as when I saw a
    naked woman
and the room stopped before it began to spin again. Slow and
    then fast
I got dizzy and did not speak and did not cry and did not cry.
She was suddenly a new kind of companion who cared for me
    and let me

see her the way she was born, naked with the soft light behind her.
    Light
fell loudly in me like water, finding all my spaces and puffing
    them up,
moving around in me. I felt a rising in my stomach
and watched her with my mouth wanting, stunned and afraid.
I moved between the pillars on the stage
to glimpse the pixies in the lights before me.
I crept close to them and asked every statement as a question
with the inflection up at the end like this: "*I am a performER
and I like to speak with othERs if I CAN?*" with the effort clear
and obvious behind my words. Sounds rose like ash choked
in my gravelly throat. I thought, "*I am a good MAN, I AM
what I always had to BE,*" and privately thanked the pixies
for what they provided me. The sideshow rehearsed
with the intense stoicism of elephants and didn't pause
other than to cackle brightly when I spoke,
no matter what I said, no matter if people thought
me different from them, no matter my biology and make-up,
no matter the dust floating or the mice feeding or the gaudy
    decoration
of a single metal chandelier with no candles. The room was lit
by the wounds of the wounded, and the light could not
    penetrate me
but emanated from the dark matter that constituted the majority
of the universe, though we do not know those elements and
    perhaps will not.
It was all we had to account for the missing mass in the orbital
    velocity
of stars that I connected on my bedroom wall. I knew the names

of the scientists of my day as they discussed with me
what the future would bring. I felt a private self inside
that I protected like a dependent embryo somewhere in my body
and it thrilled me to play the listener. Sleep was difficult.
I drew heat maps of the universe inside my embryo self
and diagramed a trajectory of growth, a small infinity. The embryo
expanded like stars, feeding the universe enough
to nearly burst walls of membranes and pulsing vessels,
merging universe with embryo and changing them, erasing both.
I actively avoided the concept of exorcism.
I wanted no part of it to touch me or be touched by me.

JOSEPH MERRICK

JOSEPH MERRICK (THE ELEPHANT MAN)

In 2010, I performed the role of John Merrick *in a production of* The Elephant Man *at the Wings Theater in New York City. The play is based on the life of a real man, Joseph Merrick, as remembered and interpreted by his doctor, Frederick Treves.*

I. New Tenderness

With his hand on my throat
        like paint on a canvas,

I am made real
to myself, witnessed

into his breath; known and knowing.

What can I do but tell him the truth
        while he watches me dress?

Say my body is the metaphor,

        a bouquet he won't stop
        flinging?

—say his hand is mine, and I
can almost breathe.

II. A Day Delivered

At first

Joseph-called-John repeats

Thank you SIR?,   a great deal.

The baths do   rid him

      of the odor.

Yes sir.   Three meals

a day delivered

      to his room.   *Yes, sir.*

A family within himself

      of other animals,   other names.

Yes.   One room.   He calls it

      home.

HOME?

III. His Other Life

For those familiar angels, the better
of them, who have let me know them, gently,
though truly I cannot know them, I reach
in my words for the grace by which they have
withstood the burning atmosphere of this
world, knowing throughout they will land harshly,
and will not be, afterward, who they were
in the moment of flight. Now looking down
at my hands, which are repositories
for the fear I have learned to love, which bear
the brutality I cannot control,
and so remind me of myself, I see
they are dripping wet. I realize my
face is dripping onto your hands too, and
the fear our hands hold is changed as I have
been changed. Listen, you who I am gripping,
you who are undoubtedly my latest
angel: release me to my other life.

IV. I Wonder Who I Am

the lover

I could not look in the face
while we fucked. The lover who

will not look at me. The women
I could not love. The women I could

not fuck. Joseph lay down on the dawn
sidewalk and kissed me, but he didn't

remember by the afternoon. Who
followed him up to that roof

when winter had barely begun to turn,
who turned to him and said

it's cold here, we'll get sick, after the sun
had risen. Joseph played a soft song.

Who let him feel it for the first time, who
was gentle. Joseph got cocktail high

and pontificated: *there are certain
someones for whom to know them is*

to love them, and Joseph had never
been touched. Who fucked his girlfriend

while her mother and Joseph both wailed
through the wall. Who took a walk to get

ice cream, came back to squad cars
and a locked bathroom door, glass broken

on the floor. Whose story is this? Who
believed in me. Who is with me now.

V. Higher

Feeling the building lean

   and stagger, Joseph-called-John sits down   in the middle

of the roof.

I am terrified, he says out loud.   I look at him.

   As a boy grows terrified,   he grows in the wrong

direction. As his   gums become inflamed,   mystified

  by his own face receding, he leans away

   from every edge and cannot stand straight.

As Joseph-called-John learns   he can try the power on,

he takes it

         for a walk. *Fuck YOU.*   Strangers scatter.

As he grows terrified of his power, and lonely without it,

   he tries to test it   against himself. And building

himself, unwieldy through years, he topples into caverns

of himself. Terrified

of the wreck, he thinks he wants

more of it. The fear on their faces

like a soothing, *like an apology*, he thinks.

They pay attention to me, they look at me seriously.

Joseph wants a higher point from which to see

but he must build it   over himself.   *Terrified*

of the ground, he climbs higher.

VI. In the Summer of My Twenty-Eighth Year

In the shower this morning,
we have a conversation
we've already had. I tell Joseph
that years ago, when I was younger,
and depended on only a handful
of visions to bring me closer
to myself, having sex

made me lonely. Of this handful
of visions, there are only one or two
that he can appreciate. Otherwise,
what is now known as his allergies
flare up. *These are the touches I need*
to feel close to myself, to say
to my deepest loneliness (bless you)

that I am here, I tell him. When I lay back
in those years, I did not need to feel close
to whoever was next to me. I needed
to feel close to Joseph; he would hover
in my brain fuzz. And when I felt
further away, because I suppose
I had somehow expected something

different, I felt my life would be
impossible. I looked at my loneliness

and could say nothing. And Joseph would
not blink. And I would be torn
between the two of them for a number
of years. Slowly, I became myself.
Slowly, still, I become myself,

wondering always with hope for who
I will be when I am older—close
and content, no distance between me
and who I want to be: a figure
and his shadow touching toes.
I will always want the impossible
tinge among the many hues.

When I am older, I will miss who I am
now, as I already miss who I was
in those years when I lay back, afraid.
When I was younger, I missed
the man I am now, not knowing who
I would become. Impossible. And I miss
the days that go by, thinking of this.

VII. Sketch for the Drunk

I turned his hips   and his hands

found the wall   so fast I thought

he was   used to me, his head

turned to me   there's a rhythm

to the memory now   it clicks

like old knees   a record finished

I go home   stand very still

in my bedroom   mirror, strip

my own hips turn   my hands

find the wall   like anything

stunned   finds aloneness

VIII. Aubade for My Almost Mugger

We are close enough   you cannot imagine
    I'm past your reach. I should've run   I haven't made it

easier for you. I'm not sure   and then
    I am. Maybe you want to do it, and can't, but I think

you have to, and you don't.   Your breath quickens,
    Joseph, and
hardens   your hands deep   in your sweatshirt pocket.

    You come closer, and like a song I'm not thinking of,
you fall away from me a bit, and come closer again,   balling
    your fists

in that sweatshirt.   Unable at last to pretend
anything else is happening,   Joseph, I think I am not alone

in doing just that.   Your eyes pummel a hole
clean through the street we walk on,   and you fill it

        with not hurting me,   then throw a match on that,
and the not hurting goes up like dry leaves.   We can smell it.

You fill the hole again, and up it goes, until we've reached
the end of the block.   Maybe you want to hurt me,
    and you are afraid.

That wouldn't change your kindness.   That's your fear, earned
someplace you know well.   Joseph, you don't mean that
    much to me.

I mean,   I don't think of you nearly as often   as I would
    otherwise,
        we both know that.   But I don't think anyone

has worked so hard not to hurt me,   worked so hard
    against their own wanting   to hurt.

As though   you are saying,   *I'm very upset with you.*

        I am going to kiss your cheek.

IX. The Dream

Halfway through the workweek

a nightmare visits me. Joseph

smirks. I remember nothing,

only that it felt like love;

the soft fullness, the knowing

never again.

Joseph makes a pot of coffee.

Steam rises from the grounds

and hangs a thin curtain

of his shadow on the ceiling.

A gray sky curls lazily

around my window, over me.

I go back to my bed, lay down

again, afraid, and wait for it.

He switches off the light.

X. For Dusk, and for Afterward

Knocking, and opening the door
        to see if you are there,
and you are. You say I'm doing
        what you have done each night.

One hand nudging the door ajar
        (Joseph's sudden face lamp-lit
from the far side of the room), one
        hand sounding softly as it swings.

Knocking, and opening the door
        to see if I am there. I am
waiting for you, close to quiet as birds
        skimming water, searching.

One wingbeat before the surface,
        then we dive. I wouldn't say so,
wouldn't say a word, if we didn't. The door
        opens. Nothing that quiet

is subliminal. When morning
        opens like a door, the bright wall
fills. The room kept still enough
        for all of us, I wait for you to wake.

Knocking, and opening the door,

the whole day does to us what we
have done to each other. I linger,
        patient as hummingbirds hanging

in air, for dusk, and for afterward.

XI. Goodness

She lies across your legs, open to the open window,
and after promising not to ask,
does not. Joseph tells you to stay, and whatever ruin

may or may not be strewn across her apartment
(ruin a made thing now
both yours and hers to keep) breathes. No after-the-fact

text, more personal than you realize or either of you
expect, in which, again,
splinters of what you feel together,

this time the underneath of it, show through,
can recompose ruin like this.

Remember, when you knelt before me, with what soft thing
I covered your eyes? And how you kept them closed, when it fell?

Thank goodness. Thank whatever you like.

XII. Skirmanté

It's dark here. We are all
full of rain here. Hold. Press

moon to night. Guess.

I see now light
opens our room (what
color?) with its curtain
and you in white clothes. I want

what you say, you to speak, *know
here*. You night-harvest rocks
your mother buried below
a field in your village, your fingers
trenched, cool wind
turns them over. Past bricks
under the grass (your name
hard in them), your grandmother's
raspberries, fresh air, yellow
wooden houses, small memorial
statues, people not breathing
but not dead, everything you
carefully dig around. Now

sleep well. Joseph and
I look for where you live.
It's dark here, *separate here.*
We are all full of rain.

XIII. Fetish

I want to be alone. A snake
rubbing its body on the ground, tasting
"I've loved you."   *I've loved you*
like I've loved highways (the endlessness),
watching highways go by,
pulling over to the side of the road,
imagining you in solitude. Our tenderness
exposed me—   *a shade*
that cannot please itself or any other.

I see myself as Lucifer, lying in your bed.
Heaven is the place I suffer
        (this is the room, these are the windows).
I dig a hole in you; I jump
        (here is the church, here is the steeple).

Shame on me.

        Joseph,   sovereign faith
in what is vulnerable, dignitary of the rocks
my heart breaks against   softening.

CAROUSELS

DESIRE

I want to be a simple man the way
my grandfather wanted to go

to sleep when the sun went down.
I want a small happiness to open
over me like a cloud, and inside

that cloud all the electricity
convulsing into a shriek of light
that is my light.

"IT WASN'T A DREAM, IT WAS A FLOOD"

— for Frank Stanford

My brother is sitting on the floor
in the corner of the kitchen
breathing really heavy,
making faces I've never seen.

The faces are taking him apart
like a cabinet.

I get him a glass of water.

He says, *I saw two people*
outside and a pig was screaming.
There were red birds everywhere.
The moon lit up the grass
and I was barefoot, running like a god
after that pig, gripping something
sharp and demented in my right hand,
seconds jumping in my head.

Water poured in from either side
like it had come down a mountain,
swept up the trees like a boy doing chores.
Before my eyes closed, I saw the pig
lifted up and spinning, already feeling everything.

MY BROTHER

True perfection seems imperfect, yet it is perfectly itself.
—Lao Tzu, translated by Stephen Mitchell

When he bursts through the door moments before dawn
and turns on all the lights, and puts on a record he loves,
when he high-fives the homeless man while sipping cider
from our Tupperware container, when he can't stand
the thought of me being angry at him, when he walks
up 6ᵗʰ Avenue the wrong way through traffic,
when he couldn't wait for his baby brother to be born,
when he tells me I am all that matters, when he autographs
the night outside the bright theater, when the word *us* closes
my eyes, scrawled thick on the lip of my bedroom shelf
as he steadies himself, looking closely at his handiwork,
when he wakes me to say I must do better by myself,
a moment he will not remember, when *us* knocks
in my mind, the poem is already written.

MY BROTHER COMES HOME

I drew on our portrait of Elvis with my silver Sharpie, filling
in his hair and his shirt collar and shoulder, leaving his pretty
face alone, and adding a speech bubble saying he loved us by
our childhood names. When you struggle mightily, you get
very gentle. I have to take myself back stronger than it took
me. I saw you dance with a man who danced with a woman,
then you danced on your own. It was theater, you were on a
stage, and I knew you'd followed me. I told you in the kitchen
that we have the same heart. I knew saying it would bring us
further into that togetherness. I could always be myself with
you, we have a secret language we don't even need. When
I asked if you still looked up to me, you looked at me and
answered *yes*. When you wrote the poem *My Brother*, I put it
in my wallet and showed it to everyone. I always wanted you
to hang out with me and my friends. You've usually been a
little ahead of where you should be. I still have that poem
in my wallet. I text you *I love you* in the middle of the night
when I haven't seen you in too long. I wanted you to stop
smoking way before you did. When our parents were gone
and I wanted to play with you, I pulled you up out of your crib
and you fell on your head. You watched me shave for the first
time and tugged on my armpit hair before you had any. I love
stepping back and thinking of you outside of my love for you.
Like how the pictures came out after we played camera tag:
your back turned, one arm reaching for the stairs mid-dash.
A wild half smile, teeth clenched in joy, takes up the whole
frame. When I'd have panic attacks, you'd sit down next to
me with a glass of water and wait. Your mouth always moved
when you were thinking hard about something, and I wanted
to know what you were saying to yourself. I love the way you

speak. You'd look out the window every car ride, and I'd have a full production going. If there was a mirror close by, I'd grab you and we'd do a music video. *Mr. President, Mr. President, it's a very important meeting,* and I'd hustle you into the next room. We laughed for a long time. We used to tape our favorite wrestling matches, then play *offense/defense,* trying to get through each other to the couch. When you wouldn't say all that much and your face didn't move, I took you aside and told you *I've seen you in worse shape.* I always told you not to go anywhere. I think I knew you thought about it, but I knew you wouldn't. We'd never leave each other. I don't know why anyone doesn't think you're awesome. I showed you the video of Tracy Chapman's show at Wembley. She had replaced Elton John, a gay black woman alone with a guitar playing songs no one had heard yet in 1988, the year you were born. I cried and cried, showing it to you. You weren't embarrassed, so neither was I. Your hands shake like mine did. Once, when I was woozy with sadness and booze, you told me *it's okay, it's all already happened.* We held each other's hands and spun in circles, spitting our drinks in each other's faces. It was ecstatic, that's how you tell it to me—I don't recall. I was always in the moment, getting lost. Slumped on New Jersey Transit going to mom's house, a stranger on the midnight platform put me on the right train. You said he was a guardian, you said *there's a difference between a talent and an artist.* Sitting in the audience at a Broadway show as kids, waiting for it to start, you knew I belonged onstage too. That's how you felt with writing and mom, I guess. You have your self-respect, and you earned a lot of it. I like that you don't usually say too much until you've been able to listen closely and think, and then you say exactly what you mean so that the person can hear it. When a bunch of my friends all left at once, by accident I said out loud *he's gonna kill my fun.* You walked over to me and hugged me in front of all of them. When my friends loved you, it made the ground feel solid, like I *knew* what I knew, and I don't always feel that way. I don't know what my life would be like without you, I really don't. It would be so empty and dumb, I wouldn't even know I was missing you. You are my bebs, this is how it is for us—it goes on and on. My brother. *Can't wait to love you forever,* we used to say. *Can you believe we get to love each other forever?*

NEWBORN

The other old men were wrong. The exact
unformable thing you know better
than to expect is here. 'Deserve' has nothing
to do with dying. Your body cooperates like a witness.

    Your mother stays up late, your father rises early.
They love going to the movies, and talking with you
    afterward. Your brother hates when anyone in the car
disagrees with his reckless devotion. You are silent,
    you will recognize this thick window as something
        formidable
to be suddenly loved, as you must suddenly break
    the water's skin to reach the actual world:

your mouth moves you talk to yourself and your cat
        creeps into your birthday shivers near you
catch someone's eyes touching like bandits touch
      a night you understand less than beautiful scenes
you'll love into years begin with hurting someone
    you can be anything you goddamn please
your thoughts don't leave as pretty as smoke
    outside a window you plant your house around
shame you don't listen to natural music
    emanating from the right hurt you become
    so thankful for a moment you forget every time
you speak the rest of your death pushes through
    porous teeth straining a leash you can chew
the sky expanding violent expanding as love
    leaves power can always go both ways
like anyone trembling the straight line

time shakes in all directions eclipsing patience
in the arms of another lover you do not
imagine even with love in front of you
there is nothing left of what you are not

even this will end you know stillness
but your hand has never been still
like anyone trying you could fall in love
with such a wonderful fool and die as undeservedly as this

the movie beginning as your brother
settles in the dust the light
turns over your father your mother speaks
late at night you hear her

your father's beard scratches your forehead

his warm face holds you   he asks   *are you*

a bad kid?

are you   going to get   close enough

to see   the whole world   as   protagonist?

when you are gone   will you find yourself

everywhere?

the previews

never end

we sit here together

the previews

never end

COMMUNICATION

Rarely does anyone say anything
they haven't said to themselves,
in words or otherwise. Joseph
Mengele drowned feeling sorry
for himself. The acrobatics
the mind performs in order
to justify the life it maintains
cannot be underestimated.
He wrote poetry pretending
to be tender. Surely even he
could not have believed himself,
so he bit the ends of his
mustache and swallowed the hair
until it congealed in his intestinal
tract. He was then too weak
to return to Germany (*where
is your empire?*). He drowned
under a different name, a fake
name chiseled in German. Exiled,
even in his diary he wrote
under a second different
name, driven by a purpose
beyond himself. Surely he spoke
to himself, too. What did he think
he was saying? Did he depend
on art to keep him company,
on words? There is hatred in places
we hold sacred. It is part
of the deal, the church, the nation
I call home, where citizens

protesting their own killers
are told *go back to Africa.*
The Nazi doctor fled to Brazil.
Some children are still
named Hitler. No one knows
where history is safe. We speak
into a void perhaps for its illusion,
so that when we speak to each other,
to animals or things, there is context
beyond ourselves, beyond mercy
and its absence.

FALLING

I imagine my mother horrified to learn I've starved myself;
my mother the stand-in for love when there is none.

Though I have hurt myself, and am angry at myself for that,
I know people don't get angry at themselves for hurting

someone they don't care about. So I am balanced, at least,
like a pendulum hung from love, falling between fear and wonder

and then the other way, and then back, and then again.

"AM I NOT CRUEL?"

The men I know
are fine thanks

and yet
you press

your cheek
against the tomb

of his chest
the men I know

answer to no one
foolhardy or otherwise

the ill advised
plans men craft

do not end
with a question

we do not disclose
what we mean

from our hands
the men I know

do not look back
upon their failures

lest they must answer
each morning the question

each long night asks of them

MY FATHER

My father, your grandfather, the youngest and only

            child in his family born in this country,

worked at a leather factory, moving up

            from the mail room to Vice President.

When I ended up in a jail cell for a night

            (before Harvard and Med School, mind you),

I knew he would be upset. My father,

            the crooner who should have been

the Jewish Sinatra (his parting song

            to the great grandchildren he knew and those

he wouldn't get the chance to meet:

            Life is just a bowl of cherries), opened his mouth

to speak, and instead began to cry, I knew

            I'd never do wrong again

if I could help it. You, son, you are a bit

different. I think you inherited that trembling.

I didn't want you to go into Tim's apartment

        after Bellevue released him. I was scared

for you. Even telling me after the fact,

        anything could've happened. Still, I was proud

you took him there, proud you went

        to him afterward, he knew you would

not shy from his hurting. Nor will you ever

        from your own. You've always known

right from wrong. It was hard to watch you

        suddenly lost and lonely, for a while. But

it was your own heart you were learning;

        that takes time. You've had to cut yourself

loose from a few bad branches. Your eyes

        got so wide when you were young. I never

knew exactly what you were thinking,

       but I trusted you. I loved taking you to school.

I told you I'd miss it, and I do. My last

       child, you kept me young, younger almost

than you sometimes seemed. *The sweet things*

       in life to you were just loaned. So how can

you lose what you never owned?

       I used to carry you everywhere. You'd run to me

like a little horse, so serious. I remember

       the first time you beat me in a race, you just kept

running.

NOTHING MOVES

—for Paneriai, 1941 – 1944

but this gold-stroked grass.
Wind in these trees,
whispering. White butterflies
landing more and more carefully.
The buried song: the song
we are born from. Light brushing
our bodies, cautious
(we stand here, still here).
Nothing but the earth moves,
alive, at least, thank god,
and time steals through us. Nothing
moves here, but what we can't see
always thrashes. If we know how
(if we can), we will bury this place
in us, careful, whispering what?
Like dandelions, we grow
toward light we never touch.
Like everything that grows.

ELEPHANT (MY BROTHER / MY HAND)

This morning, my brother and I tell each other
we are addicts. We are not resentful, we
speak openly, briefly, matter-of-fact. It's not quite
true anyways. He likes to fling himself into things,
I prefer to hurl myself out. When he calls me
from his bedroom, I know he will want to be touched—
on his outstretched arm, his side, one leg crossing
on his bed if I come to him, on mine if not.
He orders delivery, hoarse over the phone, *chicken*
lo mein. I sit on my bed and will not leave.
We kill for its tusk, we don't want to kill, we
tell ourselves. We have not had, nor have we lost,
our great chances, we tell ourselves. There is authority
within a space too pure for authority, we listen to it,
and the words undo, themselves unstitch, don't mean
too much. My kin by my side, two wandering kings,
too much wandering. The first humans in the first garden
had to have, had to say at some point, *Love's debt*
is to me, eyes caught on whichever heaven
they saw beckon like a flare, and in my vision,
the smoking gun at the end of my arm is my own hand.

LIKE MY BROTHER LOVES MUSIC

Angrier now than I've been, and clueless
with it, I tell my brother he has hurt me.

He looks at me and bears it, then puts on
a song. Music moves over us, it feels good.

I trap what hurt I have in a room. When I walk
into that room, I close the door behind me.

He rises the next morning and puts on
another song. I wake up with his music, remember

what his lush heart unfastened for mine as I drove
my lover far from the wet rage her house had become,

drove my best friend home as he confessed he loved
my lover, too. Drove myself anywhere, loving them both,

pain a part of that. The silence after everything else
is still music. I tell my brother I'm sorry, that every

moment before I tell someone I love them feels like driving
through a nighttime joy, my favorite song about to play,

that an exact silence will always lift from his music like fog,
and would be impossible without him. I tell him

I love him like angels love music, but I can't love anything that way.
Not always, not even him. I love my brother like I'd love the most

spectacular thing that ever happened to me, if that thing took human form. No, like what that thing would love the most.

THE MIRROR

—for my mother

Winter nighttime. The quiet streets swoon
with me, then hold still in the illumined snowfall.
I watch them expand and contract. A loading dock
wraps around the brick walls, its floor made of dimpled,
red-brown metal. I see the flakes of rust and light
dance. What I have always known, I am learning,
sitting with you, apart from you. I trace your words
in the air with my fingers, and our night breathes
in gusts. Holding the pages, I see where your thumb
has pressed, how brushstrokes obscure a cheekbone
into another cheekbone. New colors born along older ones
can never be alone. I have always been afraid
of what I love. Your face underneath my face. My life
a series of steps away, but I know where I'm going.
I look where you have looked. I love you that way,
among the blooms that mean the sun. Snow means
something soft falling back, like jazz, to the first melody.
The notes between home are the song. You mean you cannot
leave me, though I know you will. I watch the edge
of a lake deep enough to swallow us both.

CAROUSELS

When your bare knees together
    chatter at night, sleep an animal prayer

        that never catches you,   you
          my dimly, ever-burning, my

   reconcile, say your own name
      as I would, as I do.   As late

        as it may seem,   it is early.

We are all our own children. Some people will care for you,

        you need to let them.
   They will leave you, or you will leave them, or not.

I promise your gentleness has already lasted
   so many lives. Remember the rain

        on the back porch? You were
  small enough, then, to catch all your blessings.

I come from you as you come from me.

        Your journey is your own, and I am
          here now as your mother.

Listen   when the sky opens: *your burden*
          is your blessing. Release it.

And please care for yourself   as you would   your own beloved child.

The beginning I love you from   is everywhere.

Notes on Joseph Merrick's appearance in these poems:

Bernard Pomerance's 1977 play *The Elephant Man* and the 1980 film of the same title directed by David Lynch were based on two sources: Ashley Montagu's 1971 book *The Elephant Man: A Study in Human Dignity* and Sir Frederick Treves' 1923 account of providing medical care to Joseph Merrick, *The Elephant Man and Other Reminiscences*. Neither text considers Merrick as a person distinct from the subjective gaze of Treves and more broadly his era, and both sacrifice various facts of Merrick's life to lionize Treves. Notably, neither text uses Merrick's proper name, referring to him as "John" rather than "Joseph." Michael Howell and Peter Ford's *The True History of the Elephant Man*, published in 1980 just after the play and subsequent film were made, achieves greater three-dimensionality due to intensive research.

My relationship to Joseph Merrick was born of my experience performing the character named for him in Pomerance's play, a character consciously dramatized into artifice long after Treves first dramatized Merrick for the public's imagination and perhaps his own moral or monetary gain. For instance, Joseph himself sought out and queried showman Sam Torr in order to free himself of the Leicester Union Workhouse; he was not "found" or "discovered" as an act but in fact built his own professional life with foresight and determination. Before the police shut down the "freakshow" exhibits of London's East End, Joseph had achieved both community among his fellow performers and financial independence. During that time, Merrick was almost certainly wealthier than the vast majority of those in the audiences he faced. He made a stable foundation within the respectability politics of his time, only to see those politics mutate and destroy his living, casting him back to the brink of destitution. These facts do not fit the savior narrative put forth by Frederick Treves, who represented definitively those very respectability politics. It is untrue as well that, as Treves insisted, Joseph had never known love. Joseph, for whatever reason—and there were many to choose from—declined to provide Treves with information about his early life and childhood. In spite of his limitations, Treves seems to have been a dedicated servant to Merrick's comforts once Merrick was in his care.

Joseph Merrick was disabled; I am not. I do not wish to imply I feel any direct access to his lived experience as a disabled person by virtue of my own lived experience. When I performed the role of "John Merrick" in *The Elephant Man,* I found shelter in the character. I had over the preceding years spent significant time in hospitals due to a physical condition and had also felt emotionally alienated from the world of sensuality. This does not grant me access to Merrick's experience, and I do not claim so. Merrick was, nonetheless, a godsend avenue by which I could care for myself when it was difficult otherwise. When I was too disparaging toward myself, or felt afraid of interminable loneliness, I would think of myself performing the role of Merrick and try to take better care. I wrote these poems to be safely tender with myself, to approximate intimacy even if it was only mine. The "Joseph" who appears in this book is a Joseph Merrick of my own creation and does not attempt to honor his actual life, which I do not and cannot know. Rather, I wish to honor the grace of his presence in my imagination, a grace his documented life has afforded me. Love was all around me, just on the other side of my wanting. I've never lacked for affection and care within my family, the furthest saving grace I've known, or from friends, as he did at times.

I love Joseph Merrick, though I understand it is not Joseph Merrick, born 5 August 1862 at 50 Lee Street, Leicester, England, whom I love. I have loved the experience of performing the character named for him, which granted me the permission of tenderness within myself, and made possible my return to the world of touch. To me, he will always be possibility.

Acknowledgments

My thanks and gratitude to the following journals, in which poems or versions of poems from this book have appeared: *A Poetry Congeries, Bellevue Literary Review, Bennington Review, BOAAT, Columbia Journal, Cosmonauts Avenue, H.O.W. Journal, Horsethief, The Iowa Review, The Literary Review, The Louisville Review, Michigan Quarterly Review, Narrative* Magazine, *NECK Press, The Paris-American,* the *PEN Poetry Series, PHANTOM, The Recluse, Southword Journal, St. Petersburg Review, Tiferet Journal, Tin House,* and *Tupelo Quarterly.* Poems or versions of poems from this book were named finalists for the *Tupelo Quarterly* Poetry Prize, the *New Letters* Prize for Poetry, the Patricia Goedicke Prize in Poetry from *Cutbank Literary Journal,* the Writer's Block / Memorious Poetry Contest from *Memorious: A Journal of New Verse and Fiction, The Paris-American* Reading Series Contest, and the Marica and Jan Vilcek Prize for Poetry from *Bellevue Literary Review,* which nominated "Elephant (My Brother / My Hand)" for the Pushcart Prize. "To Be Born," "A Huge Meadow," "Love," "Dusk in Wyoming," and "Fetish," received First Place in the *Narrative* 30 Below Story and Poetry Contest from *Narrative* magazine.

My deep thanks to the Ucross Foundation, where many of these poems found breath and the foundation of this book took shape. Thank you to the Gloucester Writers Center, the New York State Summer Writers Institute, the Lacawac Artists' Residency, and New York University, for supporting my work.

I am indebted in joy to my teachers, who have shepherded my path into words. My gratitude to Henri Cole, who lit the way, to Marie Howe, who listened carefully, to Yusef Komunyakaa,

who kept the faith, to Eileen Myles, who was my example, and
to Spencer Reece, who spoke this book into existence. Thank
you to John Murillo, who believed. Thank you to Jack Gilbert,
though we never met.

To the poets in my life who safekeep and share this passion:
Alex Dimitrov, Jameson Fitzpatrick, Richie Hofmann,
Madeleine Mori, Allyson Paty, Matthew Rohrer, Danniel
Schoonebeek, Nicole Sealey, Monica Sok, Emily Jungmin
Yoon, and Javier Zamora, among so many others, thank
you. To Ann Ward and Mike Spry, my pillars of light, thank
you. To Sanaz Ghajar, Ben Hobbs, and the Built4Collapse
company, as well as the cast and crew of *The Elephant Man*,
thank you.

Thank you to the whole Summer Literary Seminars family.
Thank you to Vilnius, its Writers Union, Old Town, and
long memory. Thank you to Marius Burokas, Skirmantė
Ramoškaitė, Ieva Krivickaitė, and many more. Thank you to
the poets of Montreal and San Pedro Sula.

Thank you to Martha Rhodes and the wonderful team at
Four Way Books, who have made a dream come true.

Soren Stockman's poems have appeared in *Bellevue Literary Review*, *Bennington Review*, *BOAAT*, *Columbia Journal*, *H.O.W. Journal*, *The Iowa Review*, *The Literary Review*, *Michigan Quarterly Review*, *Narrative*, *Painted Bride Quarterly*, the *PEN Poetry Series*, *The Recluse*, *Redivider*, *St. Petersburg Review*, *Southword Journal*, *Tin House*, and *Tupelo Quarterly*, among others, while his prose has appeared in *The Fanzine*, *Kenyon Review Online*, and *Playboy*. His work was awarded First Place in the *Narrative* 30 Below Contest and was twice named a finalist for both the *New Letters* Prize for Poetry and the *Tupelo Quarterly* Poetry Prize, and has otherwise been a finalist in contests for *Bellevue Literary Review*, *Cutbank Literary Journal*, *Gulf Coast*, *Memorious*, and *The Paris-American*. Performance credits include "John Merrick" in *The Elephant Man* at the Wings Theater (2010), and more recently "Victor Pistachio" in *Bloodshot* (2020) and *Bloodshot: The Call* (2021), part of the Exponential Festival at Target Margin Theater in Brooklyn, NY. Stockman is the recipient of fellowships from the Gloucester Writers Center, the Lacawac Artists' Residency, New York University, the New York State Summer Writers Institute, and the Ucross Foundation. *Elephant* is his debut collection of poems.

Publication of this book was made possible by grants and donations. We are also grateful to those individuals who participated in our 2021 Build a Book Program. They are: Anonymous (16), Maggie Anderson, Susan Kay Anderson, Kristina Andersson, Kate Angus, Kathy Aponick, Sarah Audsley, Jean Ball, Sally Ball, Clayre Benzadón, Greg Blaine, Laurel Blossom, adam bohannon, Betsy Bonner, Lee Briccetti, Joan Bright, Jane Martha Brox, Susan Buttenwieser, Anthony Cappo, Carla and Steven Carlson, Paul and Brandy Carlson, Renee Carlson, Alice Christian, Karen Rhodes Clarke, Mari Coates, Jane Cooper, Ellen Cosgrove, Peter Coyote, Robin Davidson, Kwame Dawes, Michael Anna de Armas, Brian Komei Dempster, Renko and Stuart Dempster, Matthew DeNichilo, Rosalynde Vas Dias, Kent Dixon, Patrick Donnelly, Lynn Emanuel, Blas Falconer, Elliot Figman, Jennifer Franklin, Helen Fremont and Donna Thagard, Gabriel Fried, John Gallaher, Reginald Gibbons, Jason Gifford, Jean and Jay Glassman, Dorothy Tapper Goldman, Sarah Gorham and Jeffrey Skinner, Lauri Grossman, Julia Guez, Sarah Gund, Naomi Guttman and Jonathan Mead, Kimiko Hahn, Mary Stewart Hammond, Beth Harrison, Jeffrey Harrison, Melanie S. Hatter, Tom Healy and Fred Hochberg, K.T. Herr, Karen Hildebrand, Joel Hinman, Deming Holleran, Lillian Howan, Thomas and Autumn Howard, Catherine Hoyser, Elizabeth Jackson, Jessica Jacobs and Nickole Brown, Christopher Johanson, Jen Just, Maeve Kinkead, Alexandra Knox, Lindsay and John Landes, Suzanne Langlois, Laura Lauth, Sydney Lea, David Lee and Jamila Trindle, Rodney Terich Leonard, Jen Levitt, Howard Levy, Owen Lewis, Matthew Lippman, Jennifer Litt, Karen Llagas, Sara London and Dean Albarelli, Clarissa Long, James Longenbach, Cynthia Lowen, Ralph and Mary Ann Lowen, Ricardo Maldonado, Myra Malkin, Jacquelyn Malone, Carrie Mar, Kathleen McCoy, Ellen McCulloch-Lovell, Lupe Mendez, David Miller, Josephine Miller, Nicki Moore, Guna Mundheim, Matthew Murphy and Maura Rockcastle, Michael and Nancy Murphy, Myra Natter, Jay Baron Nicorvo, Ashley Nissler, Kimberly Nunes, Rebecca and Daniel Okrent, Robert Oldshue and

Nina Calabresi, Kathleen Ossip, Judith Pacht,
Cathy McArthur Palermo, Marcia and Chris Pelletiere,
Sam Perkins, Susan Peters and Morgan Driscoll, Patrick Phillips,
Robert Pinsky, Megan Pinto, Connie Post, Kyle Potvin,
Grace Prasad, Kevin Prufer, Alicia Jo Rabins, Anna Duke Reach,
Victoria Redel, Martha Rhodes, Paula Rhodes, Louise Riemer,
Sarah Santner, Amy Schiffman, Peter and Jill Schireson, Roni and
Richard Schotter, James and Nancy Shalek, Soraya Shalforoosh,
Peggy Shinner, Anita Soos, Donna Spruijt-Metz, Ann F. Stanford,
Arlene Stang, Page Hill Starzinger, Marina Stuart, Yerra Sugarman,
Marjorie and Lew Tesser, Eleanor Thomas, Tom Thompson and
Miranda Field, James Tjoa, Ellen Bryant Voigt, Connie Voisine,
Moira Walsh, Ellen Dore Watson, Calvin Wei, John Wender,
Eleanor Wilner, Mary Wolf, and Pamela and Kelly Yenser.